NUTRI
NINJA™

Guide to
Nutritional Goodness

75+ delicious recipes

Nutritional Analyses: Calculations for the nutritional analyses in this book are based on the largest number of servings listed within the recipes. Calculations are rounded up to the nearest gram or milligram, as appropriate. If two options for an ingredient are listed, the first one is used. Not included are optional ingredients or serving suggestions.

Editors and Content: Mona Dolgov, Laura Lagano, R.D. and Donna Shields, R.D.

Recipe Development: Shark Ninja Culinary Innovation Team and Great Flavors Recipe Development Team

Graphic Designer: Leslie Anne Feagley

Creative/Photo Director: Anne Welch

Photography: Quentin Bacon and Gary Sloan

Published in the United States of America by

Shark Ninja
180 Wells Avenue
Newton, MA, 02459

ISBN: 978-1-4675-9862-0

20 19 18 17 16

Printed in China

table of contents

your nutri ninja™...

Open the box of your Nutri Ninja™ to start on your journey toward optimal wellness!

You can now easily blend vegetables, fruits, herbs, nuts, seeds, and other nutrient-packed ingredients to create nutrient-complete juices, sauces, soups, dips, and healthier desserts.

The combination of the powerful motor and patented blade system work together to create smooth textures. Plus, this innovative combo can handle hard ingredients, such as ice, kale and fibrous greens, pulpy fruits, flaxseeds and nuts. The end result? A d........ up of nutritional goodness!

New to this? We've got you covered. Choose f........ elicious recipes. Plus, we have helpful tips and charts to ....ze your own! Our recipes include:

- high-nutrient, low-starch veg
- lower-sugar fruits
- detoxifying herbs
- forward-thinking super-food i .... s

To support your healthier lifestyle, we've crafted five wellness categories and identified key foods that can help to deliver specific health-enhancing benefits. Notes and helpful tips from our registered dietitians and nutritionists teach you about the basics of nutrient extract juicing. How much easier could it be—your daily dose of vegetables and fruits is just a few sips away.

Avocado Caesar Dressing
p. 98

4

High Sugar Content Foods

FOOD	SERVING SIZE	SUGAR (GRAMS)	FIBER (GRAMS)
Nectarine	1	11	2
Orange	1	12	3
Peach	1	12	2
Cantaloupe	1 cup	13	1
Honeydew	1 cup	14	1
Banana	1	14	3
Blueberries	1 cup	15	4
Grapes	1 cup	15	1
Pineapple	1 cup	16	2
Fig	2	16	3
Pear	1	17	6
Apple	1	19	4
Mango	1 cup	23	3
Date	2	32	3

Moderate Sugar Content Foods

FOOD	SERVING SIZE	SUGAR (GRAMS)	FIBER (GRAMS)
Sweet potato	1 cup	6	4
Blackberries	1 cup	7	8
Strawberries	1 cup	7	3
Beets	1 cup	9	4
Grapefruit	1	9	1
Tangerine	1	9	2
Watermelon	1 cup	9	1

customize your own...

Get creative with your Nutri Ninja™, and customize a healthy blend of your very own! Don't be afraid to experiment. Check out our suggestions below for creating your own signature nutrient extract juice!

To Make It Thicker

Try adding one of these ingredients for a creamier drink and to boost your nutritional intake:

- ¼ ripe banana
- 2 tablespoons avocado
- ½ tablespoon chia seeds

HOW TO MAKE A CHIA GEL: Combine 4 tablespoons of chia seeds with 2 cups of water or another liquid like coconut water. After 10 to 15 minutes, you'll have a gel! Use 1 or 2 table-spoons of gel to thicken drinks to your desired consistency. Cover and refrigerate for up to one week.

To Make It Thinner

The thickness of blended drinks depends on ice usage and whether the ingredients are fresh or frozen. To regulate the consistency of your smoothies and beverages, you can add one of these healthful ingredients to thin it down:

- 2 tablespoons green tea or chamomile tea
- 2 tablespoons coconut water
- Add a small amount of a high-moisture food, such as celery, lettuce, cucumber, lemon or lime
- Add water—important to rehydrate!
- Unsweetened almond milk adds richness, great with tropical fruits!

To Make It Sweeter

The recipes in this book are created with ingredients that are naturally low in sugar. If your taste buds require beverages that are a little sweeter, we recommend using the ingredients in the chart below.

SWEETENER	AMOUNTS	CALORIES	CHARACTERISTICS
Agave	1 tsp.	20	• Sourced from the root of the agave or yucca plant.
Dates	½ date	30	• Dried fruits provide very concentrated, natural sweetness.
Dried Figs	½ fig	30	• Dried fruits provide very concentrated, natural sweetness.
Raisins	20 raisins	30	• Dried fruits provide very concentrated, natural sweetness.
Honey	1½ tsp.	32	• Distinct rich taste—opt for raw organic honey.
Lucuma	1½ tsp.	30	• A subtropical fruit available in powder form found in most health food stores. • Fragrant, sweet and emulsifies fats if blended.
Maple Syrup	1½ tsp.	25	• Obtained from the sap of the maple tree. • Concentrated sweetness.
Stevia	½ packet	0	• An herb available in powdered or liquid form with zero calories. • Several brands of Stevia may have a slight taste difference because they are harvested from different parts of the plant.
Yacon Syrup	1½ tsp.	20	• Sourced from a South American tuber. Also available in powdered form. Sold at health food stores. • Offers half the calories of table sugar.

perfect potions

Powerhouse Combinations

Sometimes using ingredients together delivers a bigger nutritional benefit than consuming them individually. Here are a few go-together ideas for creating your own drinks that will complement your healthy eating efforts.

- Full-fat coconut milk or coconut oil + turmeric = Better utilization of turmeric's potent antioxidant compound, curcumin, aided by the fat in coconut
- Citrus + dark leafy greens = Optimal absorption of the iron in greens with the help of vitamin C–rich citrus
- Avocado or nuts + tomatoes or watermelon = Enhanced absorption of lycopene—the red-colored anti-oxidant—with the assistance of the healthy fats in avocado or nuts
- Kale or Swiss chard + strawberries = Higher availability of B vitamins found in leafy greens along with the vitamin C in berries
- Sweet potatoes or carrots + nuts = Improved absorption of fat-soluble vitamin A, contained in many orange foods, possible with the help of the healthy fats in nuts

Mix & Match Recipe Ideas

Create your own nutrient-rich juices or healthy smoothies with these great food and flavor combos!

THESE TASTE GREAT	WITH ANY OF THESE
apples, pears, nut milks	cinnamon, nutmeg, almonds, walnuts
kale, Swiss chard, romaine	fresh lemons, pears, kiwi, ginger
green tea	all berries, tart cherry and pomegranate concentrates
sweet potatoes, carrots, butternut squash	turmeric, maple syrup
arugula	mint, pears, apples
pineapple, mango, papaya	coconut, bananas
strawberries	basil, mint, goji berries

16

Gingered Acai
p. 19

nutrient-rich juices

PREP TIME: 5 minutes   YIELD: two, 11-ounce servings   CUP SIZE: 24 ounces

power ball

Blueberries are full of antioxidants and phytonutrients. Start your day off right with this luscious energy booster.

ingredients

½ ripe banana

1½ cups unsweetened coconut milk

1 teaspoon unsweetened cocoa powder

1½ cups frozen blueberries

directions

1. Place all the ingredients in the order listed into the Ninja 24-ounce cup and blend for 25 seconds.

1 SERVING: CALORIES 110; FAT 4.5G; SODIUM 10MG; POTASSIUM 240MG; CARBOHYDRATES 22G; SUGAR 13G; FIBER 5G; PROTEIN 1G; VITAMIN A 8% DV; VITAMIN C 8% DV; MAGNESIUM 10% DV; ZINC 4% DV

NINJA KNOW-HOW   ADD 1 TABLESPOON MACA POWDER FOR A SUPER FOOD BOOST.

gingered acai

Acai and pomegranate, prized for having antioxidants, plus ginger, an anti-inflammatory and great for digestion, make the perfect combination beverage for your busy day!

ingredients

½ cup unsweetened acai berry puree, thawed

1 (.035 ounce) packet stevia

2 teaspoons fresh ginger

2 cups frozen strawberries

1½ cups pomegranate juice

directions

1. Place all the ingredients in the order listed into the Ninja 24-ounce cup and blend for 25 seconds.

1 SERVING: CALORIES 190; FAT 0G; SODIUM 25MG; POTASSIUM 230MG; CARBOHYDRATES 47G; SUGAR 35G; FIBER 4G; PROTEIN 2G; VITAMIN A 2% DV; VITAMIN C 100% DV; MAGNESIUM 4% DV; ZINC 2% DV

PREP TIME: 6 minutes   **YIELD:** two, 12-ounce servings   **CUP SIZE:** 24 ounces

watermelon cooler

Freeze to a slightly slushy consistency for a low-calorie refreshing cleanser.

ingredients

¼ pear, seeded,
cut into chunks

2 large fresh basil leaves,
stems removed

2 cups chilled watermelon,
seeded, cut into chunks

directions

1. Place all the ingredients in the order listed into the Ninja 24-ounce cup and blend for 30 seconds.

1 SERVING: CALORIES 60; FAT 0G; SODIUM 0MG; POTASSIUM 200MG; CARBOHYDRATES 15G; SUGAR 12G; FIBER 1G; PROTEIN 1G; VITAMIN A 20% DV; VITAMIN C 20% DV; MAGNESIUM 4% DV; ZINC 2% DV

NINJA KNOW-HOW — ADD ⅛ TEASPOON HOLY BASIL POWDER, ALSO CALLED TULSI, FOR A SUPER FOOD BOOST.

PREP TIME: 5 minutes   YIELD: two, 10-ounce servings   CUP SIZE: 24 ounces

curry bloody mary

A Bloody Mary is a healthy vegetable treat even without alcohol. With the addition of curry spices, you get a new bright Far Eastern taste with a bunch of new phytonutrients to boot.

ingredients

1 small stalk celery, cut into chunks

½ lemon, peeled, seeded

2 small vine-ripe tomatoes
cut into quarters

⅓ cup orange carrot juice

1 teaspoon green curry paste

½ teaspoon tamarind concentrate

2 dashes hot sauce

⅛ teaspoon celery seed

1 cup ice

directions

1. Place all the ingredients in the order listed into the Ninja 24-ounce cup and blend for 30 seconds.

1 SERVING: CALORIES 50; FAT 1G; SODIUM 35MG; POTASSIUM 370MG; CARBOHYDRATES 10G; SUGAR 6G; FIBER 2G; PROTEIN 2G; VITAMIN A 90% DV; VITAMIN C 50% DV; MAGNESIUM 6% DV; ZINC 2% DV

NINJA KNOW-HOW: ADD 1 TEASPOON FRESH GINGER FOR A SUPER FOOD BOOST.

PREP TIME: 5 minutes   YIELD: two, 11-ounce servings   CUP SIZE: 24 ounces

call me popeye

Who knew green could be so yummy! A perfect smoothie filled with antioxidants!

ingredients

2 dates, cut in half

1 stalk celery, cut into quarters

1 ripe kiwi, peeled, cut in half

1 cup cabbage, chopped

1 cup kale

1⅓ cups hazelnut milk

1 cup ice

directions

1. Soak the dates in 1 cup of warm water for 30 minutes. Drain. Set aside.

2. Place all the ingredients in the order listed into the Ninja 24-ounce cup and blend for 25 seconds.

1 SERVING: CALORIES 150; FAT 3G; SODIUM 115MG; POTASSIUM 560MG; CARBOHYDRATES 29G; SUGAR 17G; FIBER 4G; PROTEIN 5G; VITAMIN A 140% DV; VITAMIN C 190% DV; MAGNESIUM 10% DV; ZINC 4% DV

PREP TIME: 6 minutes   YIELD: two, 11-ounce servings   CUP SIZE: 24 ounces

lean green ninja

The best-tasting green smoothie you will ever experience! The tropical fruit flavors mask the greens, plus you get a big boost of vitamin C.

ingredients

½ cup fresh pineapple, cut into chunks

½ cup fresh mango, cut into chunks

½ ripe banana

¼ cup packed baby spinach

¼ cup chopped kale, stems removed

½ cup water

1 cup ice

directions

1. Place all the ingredients in the order listed into the Ninja 24-ounce cup and blend for 30 seconds.

1 SERVING: CALORIES 80; FAT 0G; SODIUM 10MG; POTASSIUM 280MG; CARBOHYDRATES 19G; SUGAR 13G; FIBER 2G; PROTEIN 1G; VITAMIN A 35% DV; VITAMIN C 80% DV; MAGNESIUM 6% DV; ZINC 2% DV

 NINJA KNOW-HOW   ADD 2 TEASPOONS SPIRULINA POWDER FOR A SUPER FOOD BOOST.

PREP TIME: 6 minutes **YIELD:** two, 9-ounce servings **CUP SIZE:** 24 ounces

chocolate-coated cherry juice

Cherries have anti-inflammatory properties. The cocoa powder and avocado ingredients give this nutrient-rich juice a delicious and smooth texture.

ingredients

½ ripe avocado, pitted

1½ cups original-flavor rice milk

¾ cup frozen cherries

2 tablespoons unsweetened cocoa powder

1 (.035 ounce) packet stevia

directions

1. Place all the ingredients in the order listed into the Ninja 24-ounce cup and blend for 20 seconds.

1 SERVING: CALORIES 220; FAT 10G; SODIUM 75MG; POTASSIUM 430MG; CARBOHYDRATES 34G; SUGAR 12G; FIBER 8G; PROTEIN 3G; VITAMIN A 2% DV; VITAMIN C 70% DV; MAGNESIUM 10% DV; ZINC 4% DV

 NINJA KNOW-HOW ADD 2 TABLESPOONS TART CHERRY CONCENTRATE FOR A SUPER FOOD BOOST.

PREP TIME: 4 minutes   YIELD: two, 10-ounce servings   CUP SIZE: 24 ounces

purple potion

Beets contain many of the necessary vitamins and micronutrients that support the production and maintenance of our bodies' cells.

ingredients

¾ cup roasted beets,
cut into chunks

1 cup frozen blueberries

1¼ cups carrot juice

directions

1. Place all the ingredients in the order listed into the Ninja 24-ounce cup and blend for 25 seconds.

1 SERVING: CALORIES 130; FAT 1G; SODIUM 150MG; POTASSIUM 690MG; CARBOHYDRATES 30G; SUGAR 17G; FIBER 5G; PROTEIN 3G; VITAMIN A 570% DV; VITAMIN C 30% DV; MAGNESIUM 10% DV; ZINC 4% DV

NINJA
KNOW-HOW

ADD 2 TEASPOONS ACAI POWDER FOR A SUPER FOOD BOOST.

PREP TIME: 5 minutes   YIELD: two, 10-ounce servings   CUP SIZE: 24 ounces

pineapple pleaser

The combination of pineapple and papaya makes for a nutrient-dense drink high in vitamin C.

ingredients

¾ cup fresh, ripe papaya, peeled, cut into chunks

1¼ cups original rice milk

1 tablespoon cashew butter

1 cup frozen pineapple

directions

1. Place all the ingredients in the order listed into the Ninja 24-ounce cup and blend for 30 seconds.

1 SERVING: CALORIES 190; FAT 5G; SODIUM 95MG; POTASSIUM 230MG; CARBOHYDRATES 35G; SUGAR 20G; FIBER 2G; PROTEIN 3G; VITAMIN A 10% DV; VITAMIN C 120% DV; MAGNESIUM 10% DV; ZINC 4% DV

 NINJA KNOW-HOW | ADD 2 TABLESPOONS RAW SHELLED HEMP SEEDS FOR A SUPER FOOD BOOST.

PREP TIME: 5 minutes   YIELD: two, 11-ounce servings   CUP SIZE: 24 ounces

passion fruit power

Passion fruit is a delicious subtropical fruit that contains antioxidants, minerals, and fiber.

ingredients

1 ripe avocado, pitted, cut in half

½ cup silken tofu

⅓ cup passion fruit pulp

3 tablespoons honey

¾ cup cold water

1 cup ice

directions

1. Place all the ingredients in the order listed into the Ninja 24-ounce cup and blend for 25 seconds.

1 SERVING: CALORIES 320; FAT 17G; SODIUM 25MG; POTASSIUM 760MG; CARBOHYDRATES 44G; SUGAR 29G; FIBER 11G; PROTEIN 6G; VITAMIN A 15% DV; VITAMIN C 35% DV; MAGNESIUM 15% DV; ZINC 8% DV

NINJA KNOW-HOW   ADD 2 TEASPOONS ACAI POWDER FOR A SUPER FOOD BOOST.

PREP TIME: 5 minutes   **YIELD:** two, 9-ounce servings   **CUP SIZE:** 24 ounces

frozen kale cacao

Known as the "queen of greens," kale is recognized for its exceptional nutrient richness, many health benefits and delicious flavor.

ingredients

6 dates, cut in half

1 tablespoon unsweetened cocoa powder

1 frozen ripe banana, cut in half

1 cup chopped kale, stems removed

1⅓ cups unsweetened coconut milk

½ cup ice

directions

1. Soak the dates in 1 cup warm water for 30 minutes. Drain. Set aside.

2. Place all the ingredients in the order listed into the Ninja 24-ounce cup and blend for 45 seconds.

1 SERVING: CALORIES 170; FAT 4G; SODIUM 25MG; POTASSIUM 620MG; CARBOHYDRATES 35G; SUGAR 21G; FIBER 5G; PROTEIN 3G; VITAMIN A 70% DV; VITAMIN C 80% DV; MAGNESIUM 20% DV; ZINC 6% DV

NINJA KNOW-HOW | ADD 2 TABLESPOONS CACAO NIBS FOR A SUPER FOOD BOOST, WITH THE BENEFITS OF DARK CHOCOLATE WITHOUT SUGAR.

PREP TIME: 5 minutes   YIELD: two, 10-ounce servings   CUP SIZE: 24 ounces

carrot tip top

This is a powerhouse of vitamin A, great for vision and glowing skin!

ingredients

1¼ cups carrots, peeled, cut into chunks

1 cup carrot juice

2 tablespoons ground flaxseeds

½ cup silken tofu

1 cup ice

directions

1. Place all the ingredients in the order listed into the Ninja 24-ounce cup and blend for 45 seconds.

1 SERVING: CALORIES 150; FAT 5G; SODIUM 140MG; POTASSIUM 780MG; CARBOHYDRATES 22G; SUGAR 9G; FIBER 5G; PROTEIN 6G; VITAMIN A 720% DV; VITAMIN C 25% DV; MAGNESIUM 20% DV; ZINC 8% DV

NINJA KNOW-HOW | ADD ½ TEASPOON RED CURRY PASTE FOR A SUPER FOOD BOOST.

PREP TIME: 5 minutes   YIELD: two, 11-ounce servings   CUP SIZE: 24 ounces

you making me bananas

* *

Flaxseed milk contains no cholesterol or lactose, making it the perfect substitute for cow's milk. Banana and orange make a delicious combination for this rich, almost milkshake-like drink.

ingredients

½ orange, peeled, cut in half

1¼ cups original flax milk

½ teaspoon ground nutmeg

2 frozen ripe bananas, cut in half

¼ cup ice

directions

1. Place all the ingredients in the order listed into the Ninja 24-ounce cup and blend for 25 seconds.

1 SERVING: CALORIES 150; FAT 2G; SODIUM 50MG; POTASSIUM 480MG; CARBOHYDRATES 35G; SUGAR 22G; FIBER 4G; PROTEIN 2G; VITAMIN A 10% DV; VITAMIN C 45% DV; MAGNESIUM 10% DV; ZINC 2% DV

PREP TIME: 5 minutes   YIELD: two, 10-ounce servings   CUP SIZE: 24 ounces

quinoa-ing you up

Quinoa contains two important flavonoids, quercetin and kaempferol. We've combined the high nutrient value of old world quinoa with new world classic pumpkin pie.

ingredients

1½ cups rice milk

½ cup cooked quinoa

¾ cup pumpkin puree

¾ teaspoon pumpkin pie spice

1 tablespoon pure maple syrup

1 cup ice

directions

1. Place all the ingredients in the order listed into the Ninja 24-ounce cup and blend for 25 seconds.

1 SERVING: CALORIES 180; FAT 3.5G; SODIUM 115MG; POTASSIUM 105MG; CARBOHYDRATES 36G; SUGAR 15G; FIBER 5G; PROTEIN 4G; VITAMIN A 230% DV; VITAMIN C 2% DV; MAGNESIUM 8% DV; ZINC 4% DV

nutrient-rich juices

ginger pear defense

Ginger provides a natural anti-inflammatory and aids in digestion. Choose ripe pears for extra sweetness.

ingredients

1 ripe pear, seeded, cut into quarters

1 teaspoon fresh ginger

2¼ cups cold water

Sweetener, to taste

directions

1. Place all the ingredients in the order listed into the Ninja 24-ounce cup and blend for 20 seconds.

2. Pour mixture through a fine-mesh strainer to remove the pulp for a lighter drink.

3. Store in refrigerator for up to 3 days.

1 SERVING: CALORIES 45; FAT 0G; SODIUM 10MG; POTASSIUM 95MG; CARBOHYDRATES 11G; SUGAR 9G; FIBER 0G; PROTEIN 0G; VITAMIN A 0% DV; VITAMIN C 6% DV; MAGNESIUM 2% DV; ZINC 0% DV

PREP TIME: 6 minutes   YIELD: two, 10-ounce servings   CUP SIZE: 24 ounces

put the lime in the coconut

Low in calories, naturally fat- and cholesterol-free, and potassium-rich, coconut water is a great liquid base for healthy smoothies.

ingredients

½ cup chopped romaine lettuce

¼ green apple, seeded, cut in half

⅓ cup alfalfa sprouts

1 lime, peeled, cut in half

2 tablespoons extra-virgin raw coconut oil

½ avocado, pitted

1¼ cups coconut water

1 cup ice

directions

1. Place all the ingredients in the order listed into the Ninja 24-ounce cup and blend for 35 seconds.

1 SERVING: CALORIES 250; FAT 22G; SODIUM 170MG; POTASSIUM 710MG; CARBOHYDRATES 17G; SUGAR 7G; FIBER 7G; PROTEIN 3G; VITAMIN A 25% DV; VITAMIN C 35% DV; MAGNESIUM 15% DV; ZINC 4% DV

NINJA
KNOW-HOW
ADD 1 TABLESPOON SPANISH BEE POLLEN FOR A SUPER FOOD BOOST.

red devil

This is a healthy version of coleslaw yet low in calories.

ingredients

1 cup shredded red cabbage

¼ cup cucumber, cut in half

1 tablespoon fresh basil, stems removed

2 tablespoons pomegranate juice

1¼ cups unsweetened apple juice

½ cup silken tofu

1 cup ice

directions

1. Place all the ingredients in the order listed into the Ninja 24-ounce cup and blend for 30 seconds.

1 SERVING: CALORIES 120; FAT 2G; SODIUM 20MG; POTASSIUM 440MG; CARBOHYDRATES 24G; SUGAR 19G; FIBER 2G; PROTEIN 4G; VITAMIN A 10% DV; VITAMIN C 45% DV; MAGNESIUM 8% DV; ZINC 4% DV

NINJA **KNOW-HOW** ADD 2 TABLESPOONS TART CHERRY CONCENTRATE FOR A HIGH ANTIOXIDANT SUPER FOOD BOOST.

PREP TIME: 5 minutes   YIELD: two, 11-ounce servings   CUP SIZE: 24 ounces

coconut crush

The tart cherry concentrate makes for a high-antioxidant summertime drink.

ingredients

1 small celery stalk, cut into chunks

1 ripe banana

1¼ cups unsweetened coconut milk

1 tablespoon coconut palm sugar

1 tablespoon tart cherry concentrate

1½ cups ice

directions

1. Place all the ingredients in the order listed into the Ninja 24-ounce cup and blend for 20 seconds.

1 SERVING: CALORIES 130; FAT 3G; SODIUM 35MG; POTASSIUM 370MG; CARBOHYDRATES 28G; SUGAR 21G; FIBER 2G; PROTEIN 1G; VITAMIN A 8% DV; VITAMIN C 10% DV; MAGNESIUM 10% DV; ZINC 4% DV

NINJA KNOW-HOW ADD 1 TABLESPOON SPANISH BEE POLLEN FOR A SUPER FOOD BOOST.

PREP TIME: 5 minutes   YIELD: one, 12-ounce serving   CUP SIZE: 24 ounces

green detox splash

signature
NUTRIENT DENSE JUICE

Swiss chard is full of phytonutrients with health benefits. With the antioxidant properties of parsley, you have a winning combination. Add in sprouts, lemon and the flavor of a Golden Delicious apple, and you've made an incredibly revitalizing beverage. To create added sweetness and creaminess, include half a banana.

ingredients

1 cup chopped Swiss chard, without fibrous stalk

½ cup parsley

¼ cup alfalfa, clover, or sprouts of your choice

1 medium Golden Delicious apple, cored and cut up

2 teaspoons lemon juice

½ banana

¼ cup water

½ cup ice

directions

1. Place all the ingredients in the order listed into the Ninja 24-ounce cup and blend for 30 seconds.

1 SERVING: CALORIES 120; FAT 1G; SODIUM 100MG; POTASSIUM 540MG; CARBOHYDRATES 31G; SUGAR 20G; FIBER 7G; PROTEIN 3G; VITAMIN A 100% DV; VITAMIN C 130% DV; MAGNESIUM 15% DV; ZINC 4% DV

NINJA KNOW-HOW   ADD 1 TEASPOON GELATINIZED MACA FOR A SUPER FOOD BOOST.

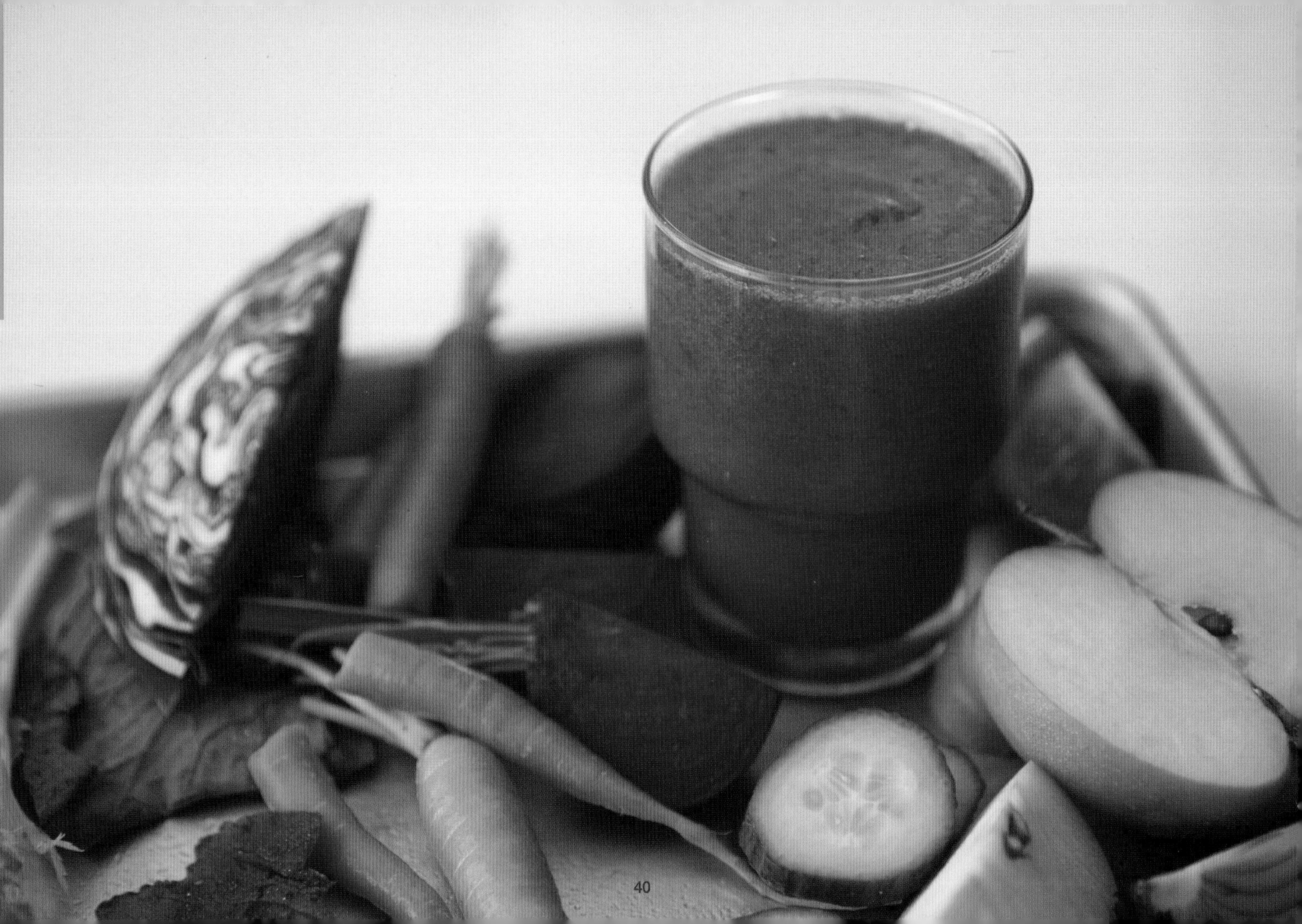

PREP TIME: 8 minutes   YIELD: two, 8-ounce servings   CUP SIZE: 24 ounces

ninja 9

signature

NUTRIENT DENSE JUICE

Eight vitamin-packed vegetables plus apple make a great combination of vitamins A, B, and C, plus a good source of fiber!

ingredients

½ cup English cucumber, cut into chunks

½ stalk celery, cut into quarters

¼ Granny Smith apple, unpeeled, cut into chunks

1 small carrot, peeled, cut into quarters

1 tablespoon red onion

¼ jalapeño, seeded

¼ cup beet, peeled

¼ cup red cabbage, shredded

¼ teaspoon kosher salt

½ cup ice

1 cup tomato, cut into quarters

directions

1. Place all the ingredients in the order listed into the Ninja 24-ounce cup and blend for 25 seconds.

1 SERVING: CALORIES 50; FAT 0G; CHOLESTEROL 0MG; SODIUM 280MG; POTASSIUM 450MG; CARBOHYDRATES 13G; SUGAR 8MG; FIBER 3G; PROTEIN 2G; VITAMIN A 100% DV; VITAMIN C 40% DV; MAGNESIUM 6% DV; ZINC 2% DV

PREP TIME: 5 minutes   YIELD: one, 12-ounce serving   CUP SIZE: 24 ounces

pear cleanse

signature

NUTRIENT DENSE JUICE

Bok choy plus cilantro can help your body's detoxifying process.

ingredients

1 cup bok choy

¼ cup cilantro

1 Bartlett pear, cored and cut up,
or ½ large Asian pear,
cored and cut up

⅛ avocado

1 teaspoon lime juice

½ date, pitted

2 ounces holy basil,
or tulsi, tea
brewed and chilled

½ cup ice

directions

1. Place all the ingredients in the order listed into the Ninja 24-ounce cup and blend for 45 seconds.

1 SERVING: CALORIES 120; FAT 0G; SODIUM 50MG; POTASSIUM 380MG; CARBOHYDRATES 28G; SUGAR 18G; FIBER 6G; PROTEIN 2G; VITAMIN A 70% DV; VITAMIN C 70% DV; MAGNESIUM 6% DV; ZINC 2% DV

NINJA KNOW-HOW ADD ½ TEASPOON FLAXSEED OIL TO ROUND OUT THE FLAVORS, BRINGING A NUTTY QUALITY WITH ADDED NUTRITION.

PREP TIME: 5 minutes   **YIELD:** one, 12-ounce serving   **CUP SIZE:** 24 ounces

ginger greens

signature

NUTRIENT DENSE JUICE

Considered two of the ultimate "detox" foods, kale and cilantro combine to cleanse your system! Avocado lends a rich, creamy consistency and a healthful dose of "good" monounsaturated fat.

ingredients

1 cup baby kale

¼ cup cilantro

¼ avocado

1 date, pitted

2 small kiwis, peeled and quartered

1 teaspoon lime juice

1 teaspoon ginger root, peeled

½ cup coconut water

⅓ cup ice

directions

1. Place all the ingredients in the order listed into the Ninja 24-ounce cup and blend for 45 seconds.

1 SERVING: CALORIES 230; FAT 9G; SODIUM 55MG; POTASSIUM 1250MG; CARBOHYDRATES 37G; SUGAR 13G; FIBER 11G; PROTEIN 7G; VITAMIN A 220% DV; VITAMIN C 440% DV; MAGNESIUM 25% DV; ZINC 8% DV

NINJA KNOW-HOW

FOR AN EXTRA DETOXIFYING BONUS, ADD ½ TEASPOON CHLORELLA POWDER

PREP TIME: 5 minutes   YIELD: one, 12-ounce serving   CUP SIZE: 24 ounces

butternut squash blast

signature
NUTRIENT DENSE JUICE

Acorn or butternut squash as a smoothie base is a unique way to use these vitamin A–rich vegetables. Paired with anti-inflammatory turmeric, cinnamon and real maple syrup, this blend seriously delivers on taste and nutrition.

ingredients

¾ cup butternut or acorn squash, seeded, peeled and oven-roasted, cooled

¾ cup vanilla almond milk, unsweetened

⅛ cup walnuts, shelled

1½ teaspoons real maple syrup

1 teaspoon ground turmeric

½ teaspoon cinnamon

½ cup ice

directions

1. Place all the ingredients in the order listed into the Ninja 24-ounce cup and blend for 30 seconds.

1 SERVING: CALORIES 220; FAT 12G; SODIUM 140MG; POTASSIUM 730MG; CARBOHYDRATES 29G; SUGAR 10G; FIBER 8G; PROTEIN 5G; VITAMIN A 350% DV; VITAMIN C 40% DV; MAGNESIUM 20% DV; ZINC 6% DV

NINJA KNOW-HOW | ADD 1 TABLESPOON OF SHELLED HEMP SEEDS TO ADD MORE PROTEIN, AND MAKE IT A MEAL!

Almond Chai Tea
p. 46

PREP TIME: 5 minutes   YIELD: two, 11-ounce servings   CUP SIZE: 24 ounces

almond chai tea

Almond chai tea, rich in antioxidants and spices, has been used for thousands of years to promote general health and well-being.

ingredients

6 dates, cut in half

¼ cup raw almonds

½ ripe banana

1½ cups chai tea, chilled, strongly brewed

directions

1. Soak the dates in 1 cup warm water for 30 minutes. Drain. Set aside.

2. Place all the ingredients in the order listed into the Ninja 24-ounce cup and blend for 45 seconds.

1 SERVING: CALORIES 180; FAT 8G; SODIUM 6MG; POTASSIUM 280MG; CARBOHYDRATES 25G; SUGAR 18G; FIBER 4G; PROTEIN 4G; VITAMIN A 0% DV; VITAMIN C 4% DV; MAGNESIUM 4% DV; ZINC 0% DV

NINJA
KNOW-HOW

ADD 1 TABLESPOON CACAO POWDER FOR A SUPER FOOD BOOST.

PREP TIME: 5 minutes   YIELD: two, 9-ounce servings   CUP SIZE: 24 ounces

tropical fruit tea

Mango, papaya and pineapple provide 100 percent of your vitamin C in this delicious nutrient-rich tea!

ingredients

½ cup ripe papaya, cut into chunks

3 dried figs

1½ cups mango passion fruit tea, strongly brewed

1 cup frozen pineapple

directions

1. Place all the ingredients in the order listed into the Ninja 24-ounce cup and blend for 25 seconds.

1 SERVING: CALORIES 90; FAT 0G; SODIUM 0MG; POTASSIUM 240MG; CARBOHYDRATES 23G; SUGAR 17G; FIBER 3G; PROTEIN 1G; VITAMIN A 8% DV; VITAMIN C 100% DV; MAGNESIUM 6% DV; ZINC 2% DV

NINJA KNOW-HOW   ADD 2 TABLESPOONS GROUND FLAXSEEDS FOR A SUPER FOOD BOOST.

PREP TIME: 5 minutes   **YIELD:** two, 11-ounce servings   **CUP SIZE:** 24 ounces

two-berry tea

A calming tea filled with berry-rich antioxidants!

ingredients

1 cup fresh blueberries

2 tablespoons goji berries

½ ripe banana

1½ cups rooibos tea, chilled, strongly brewed

1 cup ice

directions

1. Place all the ingredients in the order listed into the Ninja 24-ounce cup and blend for 30 seconds.

1 SERVING: CALORIES 100; FAT 0G; SODIUM 30MG; POTASSIUM 160MG; CARBOHYDRATES 23G; SUGAR 15G; FIBER 3G; PROTEIN 2G; VITAMIN A 2% DV; VITAMIN C 15% DV; MAGNESIUM 4% DV; ZINC 2% DV

NINJA KNOW-HOW | ADD 2 TABLESPOONS TART CHERRY CONCENTRATE FOR A SUPER FOOD BOOST.

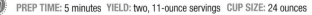

PREP TIME: 5 minutes   **YIELD:** two, 11-ounce servings   **CUP SIZE:** 24 ounces

green tea detox tonic

Green tea is an incredible detoxifying agent, whether hot or cold.

ingredients

1 cup red leaf lettuce

¼ cup cucumber, cut in half

2 (.035 ounce) packets stevia

1½ cups green tea, strongly brewed

1 cup frozen mixed berries

directions

1. Place all the ingredients in the order listed into the Ninja 24-ounce cup and blend for 30 seconds.

1 SERVING: CALORIES 35; FAT 0G; SODIUM 0MG; POTASSIUM 110MG; CARBOHYDRATES 10G; SUGAR 6G; FIBER 2G; PROTEIN 1G; VITAMIN A 20% DV; VITAMIN C 15% DV; MAGNESIUM 0% DV; ZINC 0% DV

 NINJA KNOW-HOW ADD 1 TABLESPOON ALOE VERA JUICE FOR A SUPER FOOD BOOST.

PREP TIME: 5 minutes   YIELD: two, 10-ounce servings   CUP SIZE: 24 ounces

cherry dragon tea

Cherries contain melatonin, an antioxidant that is necessary for restful sleep.

ingredients

1½ cups cherry tea, strongly brewed

¼ teaspoon rose water

2 tablespoons honey

1¼ cups frozen dark sweet cherries

directions

1. Place all the ingredients in the order listed into the Ninja 24-ounce cup and blend for 25 seconds.

1 SERVING: CALORIES 120; FAT 0G; SODIUM 0MG; POTASSIUM 220MG; CARBOHYDRATES 31G; SUGAR 27G; FIBER 2G; PROTEIN 1G; VITAMIN A 2% DV; VITAMIN C 2% DV; MAGNESIUM 0% DV; ZINC 0% DV

NINJA KNOW-HOW

ADD 2 TEASPOONS ACAI POWDER FOR A SUPER FOOD BOOST.

PREP TIME: 4 minutes   YIELD: two, 9-ounce servings   CUP SIZE: 24 ounces

ginger peach lemonade

* *

A refreshing summer lemonade with the addition of phytochemical-rich peaches. A simple blend of happiness.

ingredients

2 cups lemonade

1⅓ cups frozen peach slices

1 teaspoon fresh ginger

Sweetener, to taste

directions

1. Place all the ingredients in the order listed into the Ninja 24-ounce cup and blend for 25 seconds.

1 SERVING: CALORIES 130; FAT 0G; SODIUM 10MG; POTASSIUM 160MG; CARBOHYDRATES 35G; SUGAR 32G; FIBER 1G; PROTEIN 1G; VITAMIN A 6% DV; VITAMIN C 160% DV; MAGNESIUM 2% DV; ZINC 0% DV

PREP TIME: 5 minutes **YIELD:** two, 12-ounce servings **CUP SIZE:** 24 ounces

apple, spice 'n everything nice

A delicious tea that has the great flavors of your favorite fall apple crisp!

ingredients

¼ cup golden raisins

½ red apple, seeded, cut in half

2 (.035 ounce) packets stevia

1½ cups apple tea,
strongly brewed

1 cup ice

directions

1. Place the raisins in a container and add ½ cup water. Cover and place in the refrigerator overnight to soak. Drain raisins after soaking.

2. Place the soaked raisins with the rest of the ingredients in the order listed into the Ninja 24-ounce cup and blend for 30 seconds.

1 SERVING: CALORIES 90; FAT 0G; SODIUM 10MG; POTASSIUM 240MG; CARBOHYDRATES 22G; SUGAR 19G; FIBER 2G; PROTEIN 1G; VITAMIN A 0% DV; VITAMIN C 4% DV; MAGNESIUM 0% DV; ZINC 0% DV

NINJA KNOW-HOW ADD 2 TABLESPOONS MACA POWDER FOR A SUPER FOOD BOOST.

53

PREP TIME: 5 minutes **YIELD:** two, 10-ounce servings **CUP SIZE:** 24 ounces

coconut mango energyade

Create your own natural sports drink for active adults and children. High in potassium and perfect for hydration!

ingredients

¾ cup fresh chopped ripe mango

½ cup fresh mint

2¼ cups coconut water

directions

1. Place all the ingredients in the order listed into the Ninja 24-ounce cup and blend for 20 seconds.

2. Store in refrigerator for up to 3 days.

1 SERVING: CALORIES 80; FAT 0G; SODIUM 15MG; POTASSIUM 630MG; CARBOHYDRATES 20G; SUGAR 17G; FIBER 0G; PROTEIN 1G; VITAMIN A 15% DV; VITAMIN C 40% DV; MAGNESIUM 2% DV; ZINC 0% DV

pineapple mint water

....

Mint is a proven stomach soother and is great for your breath, too.

ingredients

½ cup fresh pineapple chunks

1 teaspoon fresh mint,
stems removed

2¼ cups cold water

Sweetener, to taste

directions

1. Place all the ingredients in the order listed into the Ninja 24-ounce cup and blend for 20 seconds.

2. Pour mixture through a fine-mesh strainer to extract the flavored water.

3. Store in refrigerator for up to 3 days.

1 SERVING: CALORIES 20; FAT 0G; SODIUM 10MG; POTASSIUM 45MG; CARBOHYDRATES 5G; SUGAR 4G; FIBER 0G; PROTEIN 0G; VITAMIN A 0% DV; VITAMIN C 35% DV; MAGNESIUM 2% DV; ZINC 0% DV

PREP TIME: 5 minutes YIELD: two, 11-ounce servings CUP SIZE: 24 ounces

strawberry basil water

Know as the "royal herb" in France, basil contains a wide range of essential oils and is rich in flavonoids and anthocyanins with many antioxidant benefits.

ingredients

1 cup fresh strawberries, tops removed

¼ cup packed fresh basil, stems removed

2 cups cold water

Sweetener, to taste

directions

1. Place all the ingredients in the order listed into the Ninja 24-ounce cup and blend for 20 seconds.

2. Pour mixture through a fine-mesh strainer to extract the flavored water.

3. Store in refrigerator for up to 3 days.

1 SERVING: CALORIES 20; FAT 0G; SODIUM 10MG; POTASSIUM 130MG; CARBOHYDRATES 4G; SUGAR 4G; FIBER 0G; PROTEIN 1G; VITAMIN A 6% DV; VITAMIN C 80% DV; MAGNESIUM 4% DV; ZINC 2% DV

PREP TIME: 5 minutes **YIELD:** two, 10-ounce servings **CUP SIZE:** 24 ounces

vanilla orange water

* *

Just a hint of vanilla and orange makes this water-based drink a healthier, low-calorie alternative, and a great way to stay hydrated!

ingredients

½ medium orange, peeled, cut in half

⅛ teaspoon pure vanilla extract

2¼ cups cold water

Sweetener, to taste

directions

1. Place all the ingredients in the order listed into the Ninja 24-ounce cup and blend for 20 seconds.

2. Pour mixture through a fine-mesh strainer to extract the flavored water.

3. Store in refrigerator for up to 3 days.

1 SERVING: CALORIES 15; FAT 0G; SODIUM 10MG; POTASSIUM 60MG; CARBOHYDRATES 3G; SUGAR 3G; FIBER 0G; PROTEIN 0G; VITAMIN A 2% DV; VITAMIN C 30% DV; MAGNESIUM 2% DV; ZINC 0% DV

infused teas & waters

PREP TIME: 5 minutes   YIELD: two, 9-ounce servings   CUP SIZE: 24 ounces

grape apple water

The light crisp taste of green apple and green grapes will make this a refreshing beverage!

ingredients

1 cup green grapes, stems removed

½ green apple, seeded, cut in half

1½ cups cold water

Sweetener, to taste

directions

1. Place all the ingredients in the order listed into the Ninja 24-ounce cup and blend for 20 seconds.

2. Pour mixture through a fine-mesh strainer to extract the flavored water.

3. Store in refrigerator for up to 3 days.

1 SERVING: CALORIES 70; FAT 0G; SODIUM 10MG; POTASSIUM 190MG; CARBOHYDRATES 18G; SUGAR 16G; FIBER 0G; PROTEIN 1G; VITAMIN A 2% DV; VITAMIN C 8% DV; MAGNESIUM 2% DV; ZINC 0% DV

Trail Mix in a Glass
p. 61

PREP TIME: 7 minutes   YIELD: two, 11-ounce servings   CUP SIZE: 24 ounces

coffee soymoothie

This creamy coffee drink has both almond butter and silken tofu to get you started in the morning!

ingredients

1 cup strongly brewed decaf coffee

¾ cup silken tofu

1 tablespoon almond butter

¼ teaspoon cardamom powder

2 tablespoons agave nectar

1 cup ice

directions

1. Place all the ingredients in the order listed into the Ninja 24-ounce cup and blend for 20 seconds.

1 SERVING: CALORIES 160; FAT 7G; SODIUM 25MG; POTASSIUM 300MG; CARBOHYDRATES 19G; SUGAR 15G; FIBER 1G; PROTEIN 6G; VITAMIN A 0% DV; VITAMIN C 0% DV; MAGNESIUM 15% DV; ZINC 6% DV

PREP TIME: 7 minutes   YIELD: two, 11-ounce servings   CUP SIZE: 24 ounces

trail mix in a glass

Great for those with an active lifestyle, all the flavors of a trail mix whipped up in a nourishing breakfast.

ingredients

¼ cup raw unsalted almonds

¼ cup raw unsalted pumpkin seeds

1 tablespoon raw sesame seeds

¼ cup goji berries

¼ cup pomegranate juice concentrate

1¼ cups unsweetened almond milk

3 tablespoons honey

1 cup ice

directions

1. Place all the ingredients in the order listed into the Ninja 24-ounce cup and blend for 25 seconds.

1 SERVING: CALORIES 450; FAT 24G; SODIUM 200MG; POTASSIUM 470MG; CARBOHYDRATES 47G; SUGAR 35G; FIBER 5G; PROTEIN 13G; VITAMIN A 10% DV; VITAMIN C 2% DV; MAGNESIUM 45% DV; ZINC 4% DV

NINJA KNOW-HOW   ADD 1 TABLESPOON SPANISH BEE POLLEN FOR A SUPER FOOD BOOST.

PREP TIME: 7 minutes   YIELD: two, 11-ounce servings   CUP SIZE: 24 ounces

strawberry sin-sation

With an amazing combination of antioxidant fruits and digestive herbs, this delicious nutrient extract juice is so refreshing.

ingredients

1½ cups fresh strawberries, cut in quarters, stems removed

1 tablespoon fresh mint, stems removed

1 teaspoon fresh ginger

1 tablespoon unsalted sunflower seeds

¾ cup pomegranate juice

½ cup coconut water

½ cup ice

directions

1. Place all the ingredients in the order listed into the Ninja 24-ounce cup and blend for 25 seconds.

1 SERVING: CALORIES 130; FAT 3G; SODIUM 75MG; POTASSIUM 650MG; CARBOHYDRATES 26G; SUGAR 20G; FIBER 4G; PROTEIN 3G; VITAMIN A 2% DV; VITAMIN C 120% DV; MAGNESIUM 15% DV; ZINC 4% DV

PREP TIME: 6 minutes   YIELD: two, 11-ounce servings   CUP SIZE: 24 ounces

orange sunshine splash

Add some tofu protein and antioxidant "goji power" to your morning OJ for a silky smoothie!

ingredients

¾ cup silken tofu

¼ cup goji berries

1 orange, peeled, cut in half

¼ cup orange juice

2 (.035 ounce) packets stevia

1 cup ice

directions

1. Place all the ingredients in the order listed into the Ninja 24-ounce cup and blend for 30 seconds.

1 SERVING: CALORIES 150; FAT 2.5G; SODIUM 60MG; POTASSIUM 360MG; CARBOHYDRATES 24G; SUGAR 17G; FIBER 3G; PROTEIN 7G; VITAMIN A 8% DV; VITAMIN C 80% DV; MAGNESIUM 8% DV; ZINC 4% DV

NINJA KNOW-HOW ADD ¼ CUP ALOE VERA JUICE FOR A SUPER FOOD BOOST.

breakfast

buckwheat boost pancakes

• •

Serve pancakes with fresh fruit instead of syrup for a healthier option!

ingredients

1 cup buttermilk

1 egg

3 tablespoons canola oil

½ cup buckwheat flour

½ cup all-purpose flour

1 teaspoon baking soda

1 teaspoon sugar

½ teaspoon salt

1 tablespoon honey

directions

1. Place the buttermilk, egg and canola oil into the Ninja 24-ounce cup and blend for 5 seconds. Add the rest of the ingredients except for the honey, and blend for 5 seconds. Add the honey, and blend for 5 more seconds.

2. Let batter set for 1 hour.

3. On a lightly oiled griddle or sauté pan over medium heat, pour pancake batter in desired size and cook until small bubbles form. Flip and continue cooking until center is puffed and springs back when gently pushed.

1 SERVING: CALORIES 290; FAT 12G; SODIUM 470MG; POTASSIUM 180MG; CARBOHYDRATES 40G; SUGAR 11G; FIBER 3G; PROTEIN 7G; VITAMIN A 4% DV; VITAMIN C 0% DV; MAGNESIUM 15% DV; ZINC 8% DV

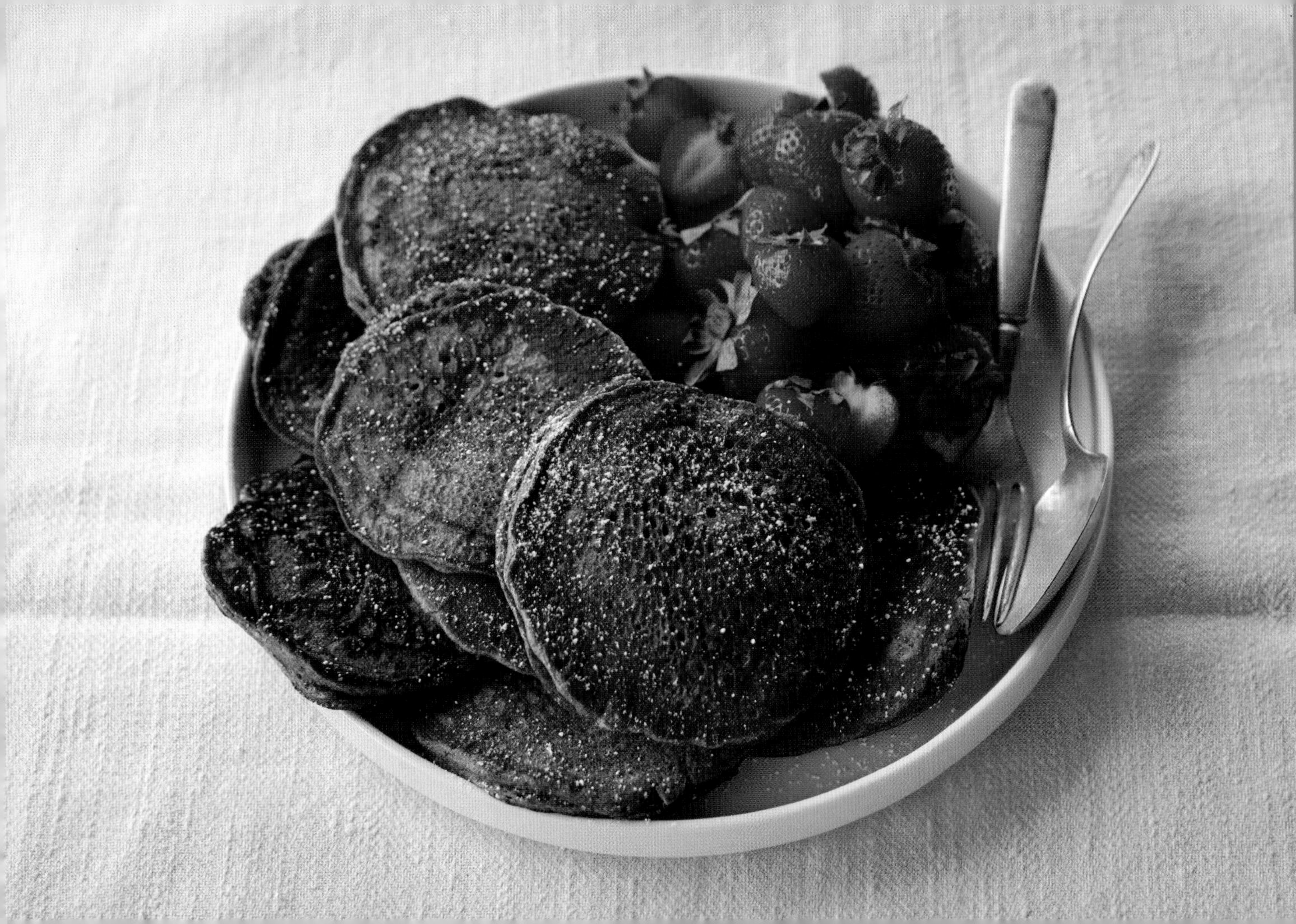

breakfast

banana sweet potato blast

Sweet potatoes are rich in vitamin A, and provide a very satisfying meal.

ingredients

6 dates, cut in half

¾ cup sweet potatoes, peeled,
cut into quarters

1 ripe banana, cut in half

¼ teaspoon ground nutmeg

1 cup skim milk

1 cup ice

directions

1. Soak the dates in 1 cup warm water for 30 minutes. Drain. Set aside.

2. Place the sweet potatoes with 3 cups of water into a small saucepan over medium heat and cook until fork-tender. Drain, then cool completely. Set aside.

3. Place all the ingredients in the order listed into the Ninja 24-ounce cup and blend for 25 seconds.

1 SERVING: CALORIES 200; FAT .5G; SODIUM 85MG; POTASSIUM 710MG; CARBOHYDRATES 46G; SUGAR 29G; FIBER 5G; PROTEIN 6G; VITAMIN A 140% DV; VITAMIN C 10% DV; MAGNESIUM 15% DV; ZINC 6% DV

NINJA
KNOW-HOW

ADD 1 TABLESPOON
FLAXSEEDS FOR A SUPER
FOOD BOOST.

PREP TIME: 5 minutes   **YIELD:** two, 11-ounce servings   **CUP SIZE:** 24 ounces

the sunflower

· ·

Sunflower butter delivers omega-3 fats and proteins, making this a satisfying on-the-go breakfast or snack.

ingredients

1 ripe banana, cut in half

1¼ cups unsweetened vanilla almond milk

¼ cup sunflower butter

¼ teaspoon ground cinnamon

1 tablespoon pure maple syrup

1 cup ice

directions

1. Place all the ingredients in the order listed into the Ninja 24-ounce cup and blend for 25 seconds.

1 SERVING: CALORIES 300; FAT 20G; SODIUM 220MG; POTASSIUM 540MG; CARBOHYDRATES 29G; SUGAR 17G; FIBER 4G; PROTEIN 7G; VITAMIN A 8% DV; VITAMIN C 10% DV; MAGNESIUM 30% DV; ZINC 10% DV

NINJA KNOW-HOW SUBSTITUTE 2 TABLESPOONS LUCUMA POWDER IN PLACE OF PURE MAPLE SYRUP FOR A SUPER FOOD BOOST.

top o' the mornin' smoothie

A perfect on-the-go breakfast filled with protein, potassium and Vitamin C!

ingredients

1 banana, peeled

1 orange, peeled, cut in half

1 cup vanilla almond milk

½ teaspoon ground cinnamon

1 scoop whey protein powder

½ cup ice

directions

1. Place all the ingredients in the order listed above into the Ninja 24-ounce cup and blend for 30 seconds.

1 SERVING: CALORIES 240; FAT 2G; SODIUM 112 MG; POTASSIUM 335 MG; CARBOHYDRATES 17 G; SUGAR 9 G; FIBER 3 G; PROTEIN: 9 G VITAMIN A: 6% DV VITAMIN C 20% DV MAGNESIUM 6% DV; ZINC 0% DV

breakfast

strawberry protein power

• •

A totally new twist on a strawberry smoothie with protein-packed tofu.

ingredients

⅔ cup silken tofu

1 cup frozen strawberries

2 tablespoons honey

1¼ cups original almond milk

directions

1. Place all the ingredients in the order listed into the Ninja 24-ounce cup and blend for 35 seconds.

1 SERVING: CALORIES 150; FAT 4G; SODIUM 115MG; POTASSIUM 400MG; CARBOHYDRATES 26G; SUGAR 20G; FIBER 2G; PROTEIN 5G; VITAMIN A 6% DV; VITAMIN C 50% DV; MAGNESIUM 15%; ZINC 4% DV

PREP TIME: 6 minutes   YIELD: two, 11-ounce servings   CUP SIZE: 24 ounces

raspberry almond butter shake

Nutrient-dense raspberries combine beautifully with heart-healthy almond butter, which is rich in healthier monounsaturated fats.

ingredients

1 tablespoon chia seeds

3 dates, cut in half

½ teaspoon pure vanilla extract

2 tablespoons almond butter

1¼ cups unsweetened almond milk

1 cup frozen raspberries

directions

1. Place the chia seeds in a container and add ½ cup water. Cover and place in the refrigerator overnight to soak.

2. Soak the dates in 1 cup warm water for 30 minutes. Drain. Set aside.

3. Place the soaked chia seeds, the dates and the rest of the ingredients in the order listed into the Ninja 24-ounce cup and blend for 40 seconds.

1 SERVING: CALORIES 200; FAT 12G; SODIUM 150MG; POTASSIUM 390MG; CARBOHYDRATES 21G; SUGAR 10G; FIBER 7G; PROTEIN 5G; VITAMIN A 6% DV; VITAMIN C 15% DV; MAGNESIUM 20% DV; ZINC 6% DV

NINJA KNOW-HOW ADD 2 TEASPOONS ACAI POWDER FOR A HIGH ANTIOXIDANT SUPER FOOD BOOST.

PREP TIME: 5 minutes   **YIELD:** two, 11-ounce servings   **CUP SIZE:** 24 ounces

cinnamon toast

• •

The positive health effects of chia seeds include boosting energy and aiding digestion. They are also a wonderful natural thickener for creating a creamy, shake-like texture in any smoothie.

ingredients

1 tablespoon chia seeds

¼ cup raisins

1¼ cups unsweetened vanilla almond milk

¾ teaspoon ground cinnamon

3 tablespoons vanilla whey protein powder

1 cup ice

directions

1. Place the chia seeds in a container and add ½ cup water. Cover and place in the refrigerator overnight to soak.

2. Place the raisins in a container and add ½ cup water. Cover and place in the refrigerator overnight to soak. Drain raisins after soaking.

3. Place the soaked chia seeds and raisins with the rest of the ingredients in the order listed into the Ninja 24-ounce cup and blend for 40 seconds.

1 SERVING: CALORIES 160; FAT 4.5G; SODIUM 140MG; POTASSIUM 350MG; CARBOHYDRATES 19G; SUGAR 11G; FIBER 4G; PROTEIN 11G; VITAMIN A 6% DV; VITAMIN C 0% DV; MAGNESIUM 8% DV; ZINC 2% DV

NINJA KNOW-HOW : ADD 2 TABLESPOONS MACA POWDER FOR A SUPER FOOD BOOST.

Curried Carrot Soup
p. 82

soups & entrées

PREP TIME: 4 minutes   **YIELD:** two, 10-ounce servings   **CUP SIZE:** 24 ounces

waldorf salad

* *

A tried-and-true favorite salad turned into an easy and healthy on-the-go meal!

ingredients

1 cup chopped romaine
lettuce

⅓ cup raw walnut halves

1¼ cups frozen red grapes

1¼ cups water

directions

1. Place all the ingredients in the order listed into the Ninja 24-ounce cup and blend for 35 seconds.

1 SERVING: CALORIES 200; FAT 13G; SODIUM 10MG; POTASSIUM 320MG; CARBOHYDRATES 21G; SUGAR 15G; FIBER 3G; PROTEIN 4G; VITAMIN A 40% DV; VITAMIN C 8% DV; MAGNESIUM 10% DV; ZINC 4% DV

PREP TIME: 5 minutes **YIELD:** two, 10-ounce servings **CUP SIZE:** 24 ounces

salad on the go

• •

Kombucha provides probiotics that aid digestion and possibly even supports the immune system. It is available as a drink in the refrigerated section of most supermarkets.

ingredients

½ ripe pear, seeded, cut in half

1 tablespoon mint, stems removed

1 cup baby arugula

1 cup original-flavor kombucha

1 cup ice

directions

1. Place all the ingredients in the order listed into the Ninja 24-ounce cup and blend for 25 seconds.

1 SERVING: CALORIES 45; FAT 0G; SODIUM 10MG; POTASSIUM 95MG; CARBOHYDRATES 11G; SUGAR 6G; FIBER 2G; PROTEIN 0G; VITAMIN A 6% DV; VITAMIN C 6% DV; MAGNESIUM 2% DV; ZINC 0% DV

 NINJA **KNOW-HOW** | ADD 2 TEASPOONS SPIRULINA FOR A HIGH-ENERGY SUPER FOOD BOOST.

chicken pita sandwich

An easy, high-protein dinner in less than 30 minutes with scrumptious, ethnic flavors.

ingredients

2 tablespoons tandoori marinade
(see recipe on page 100)

3 tablespoons cucumber feta dip
(see recipe on page 86)

8 ounces raw chicken breast, cut
into 2-inch pieces

2 8-inch whole wheat pita bread
rounds

2 vine-ripe tomatoes

8 Boston lettuce leaves

directions

1. Marinate the chicken breast pieces in the tandoori marinade for 2 hours.

2. Place the marinated chicken breast pieces into the Ninja 18-ounce cup and pulse 5 or 7 times.

3. Lightly coat a nonstick skillet with cooking spray. Over medium heat, sauté the chicken mixture until cooked, about 4 minutes.

4. To assemble sandwich, cut pita bread rounds in half, open the pocket, place the lettuce and tomato and evenly divide the cucumber feta dip and cooked ground chicken into the pockets.

PREP TIME: 15 minutes   **COOK TIME:** 35 minutes   **YIELD:** 2 servings   **CUP SIZE:** 24 ounces

beet soup

Beet soup is a unique source of phytonutrients that may help provide antioxidant and anti-inflammatory support.

ingredients

2 teaspoons extra-virgin olive oil

1 garlic clove, peeled, chopped

¼ small yellow onion, chopped

1 celery stalk, chopped

¼ cup chopped sweet potato

1 medium beet, peeled, chopped

¼ teaspoon kosher salt

⅛ teaspoon ground black pepper

1⅔ cups unsalted vegetable stock

directions

1. Preheat a 3-quart sauce pot on medium-low heat. Add the oil, garlic, onions and celery and sauté, stirring, until the onions are translucent and the celery soft, approximately 5 to 7 minutes.

2. Add the sweet potato, beet, salt, black pepper and vegetable stock. Bring to a boil, reduce the heat to medium-low and cook for 30 to 35 minutes or until the beets are fork-tender.

3. Remove from the heat and cool to room temperature.

4. In the Ninja 24-ounce cup, blend the soup mixture for 30 seconds.

5. Return to the pot and simmer until heated.

1 SERVING: CALORIES 90; FAT 5G; SODIUM 490MG;
POTASSIUM 230MG; CARBOHYDRATES 11G; SUGAR 6G;
FIBER 3G; PROTEIN 1G; VITAMIN A 50% DV; VITAMIN C 6% DV;
MAGNESIUM 4% DV; ZINC 2% DV

PREP TIME: 10 minutes YIELD: 2 servings CUP SIZE: 24 ounces

cucumber avocado soup

Cucumbers are a source of B vitamins. Jalapeño, cilantro, and lemon pack this refreshing soup with additional vitamin C and phytonutrients.

ingredients

1 avocado, pitted, cut into quarters

¼ yellow pepper, seeded, chopped

½ jalapeño, seeded, cut in half

¼ cup packed fresh cilantro, stems removed

1 garlic clove, peeled

½ teaspoon kosher salt

1 tablespoon freshly squeezed lemon juice

1⅛ cups unsalted chicken stock

1¼ cups chopped English cucumber

directions

1. Place all the ingredients in the order listed into the Ninja 24-ounce cup and blend for 35 seconds.

2. Chill before serving.

1 SERVING: CALORIES 190; FAT 15G; SODIUM 620MG; POTASSIUM 650MG; CARBOHYDRATES 15G; SUGAR 4G; FIBER 8G; PROTEIN 3G; VITAMIN A 8% DV; VITAMIN C 80% DV; MAGNESIUM 10% DV; ZINC 6% DV

PREP TIME: 15 minutes COOK TIME: 35 minutes YIELD: 4 servings CUP SIZE: 24 ounces

kale and celery root soup

This soup only has 60 calories per servings! It's also extremely nutrient-rich! Here's to your health!

ingredients

2 teaspoons extra-virgin olive oil

1 garlic clove, peeled, chopped

½ small yellow onion, chopped

½ bulb celery root (2½ ounces), peeled, cut into 1-inch pieces

3 ounces kale, chopped

1 teaspoon kosher salt

¼ teaspoon ground black pepper

4 cups unsalted vegetable stock

directions

1. Preheat a 5-quart sauce pot on medium-low heat. Add the oil, garlic and onions and sauté, gently stirring, for about 3 to 5 minutes or until translucent.

2. Add the remaining ingredients. Bring to a boil, reduce the heat to medium-low and cook for 20 to 25 minutes or until the celery root is fork-tender.

3. Remove from the heat and cool to room temperature.

4. In the Ninja 24-ounce cup, blend the soup mixture in two batches for 25 to 30 seconds.

5. Return to pot and simmer until heated.

1 SERVING: CALORIES 60; FAT 2.5G; SODIUM 750MG; POTASSIUM 170MG; CARBOHYDRATES 8G; SUGAR 3G; FIBER 2G; PROTEIN 1G; VITAMIN A 45% DV; VITAMIN C 45% DV; MAGNESIUM 4% DV; ZINC 2% DV

PREP TIME: 15 minutes **COOK TIME:** 30 minutes **YIELD:** 2 servings **CUP SIZE:** 24 ounces

curried carrot soup

This delicious beta-carotene-rich carrot soup is fantastic with the added Indian flavor.

ingredients

2 teaspoons extra-virgin olive oil

2 garlic cloves, peeled, chopped

½ medium yellow onion, chopped

¼ teaspoon kosher salt

¼ teaspoon ground black pepper

1 teaspoon red curry paste

1½ cups chopped carrots

1¼ cups unsalted chicken stock

1 cup light coconut milk

directions

1. Preheat a 3-quart saucepan on medium-low heat. Add the oil and sauté the garlic and onions for 3 to 5 minutes, stirring until translucent.

2. Add the salt, black pepper, red curry paste, carrots, and chicken stock. Bring to a boil, reduce the heat to medium-low, and cook for 20 to 25 minutes or until the carrots are fork-tender.

3. Remove from the heat, add the coconut milk and cool to room temperature.

4. In the Ninja 24-ounce cup, blend the soup mixture in two batches for 25 to 30 seconds.

5. Return to the saucepan and simmer until heated.

1 SERVING: CALORIES 190; FAT 14G; SODIUM 480MG; POTASSIUM 350MG; CARBOHYDRATES 16G; SUGAR 7G; FIBER 4G; PROTEIN 1G; VITAMIN A 320% DV; VITAMIN C 15% DV; MAGNESIUM 4% DV; ZINC 2% DV

PREP TIME: 15 minutes COOK TIME: 35 minutes YIELD: 2 servings CUP SIZE: 24 ounces

white bean & cabbage soup

This proven taste combination of beans and veggies is a protein-rich meal. If you want more protein, add some sautéed shrimp or chicken.

ingredients

2 teaspoons extra-virgin olive oil

1 garlic clove, peeled, chopped

1 small yellow onion, chopped

1 celery stalk, chopped

⅓ cup chopped green pepper

2 cups chopped green cabbage

½ teaspoon kosher salt

¼ teaspoon ground black pepper

⅛ teaspoon dried oregano leaves

3 cups unsalted vegetable stock

1 15-ounce can cannellini beans, drained, rinsed

directions

1. In a 3-quart sauce pot at medium-low heat, add the oil, garlic, onions, celery and green pepper. Cook for 7 minutes.

2. Add the green cabbage, salt, black pepper, oregano and vegetable stock. Bring to a boil, reduce the heat to medium-low and cook for 30 to 35 minutes.

3. Remove from the heat and cool to room temperature.

4. In the Ninja 24-ounce cup, blend the soup mixture for 25 seconds.

5. Return to the pot, add the cannellini beans and simmer until heated.

1 SERVING: CALORIES 270; FAT 6G; SODIUM 1200MG; POTASSIUM 280MG; CARBOHYDRATES 44G; SUGAR 7G; FIBER 13G; PROTEIN 10G; VITAMIN A 15% DV; VITAMIN C 70% DV; MAGNESIUM 6% DV; ZINC 2% DV

PREP TIME: 15 minutes   COOK TIME: 30 minutes   YIELD: 2 servings   CUP SIZE: 24 ounces

creamy sweet potato soup

A vegan creamy soup without the added fat of heavy cream.

ingredients

1 tablespoon extra-virgin olive oil

½ medium yellow onion, chopped

½ teaspoon kosher salt

¼ teaspoon ground black pepper

2 cups 1-inch cubes sweet potatoes

1½ cups unsalted vegetable stock

½ cup silken tofu, drained

directions

1. Preheat a 3-quart sauce pot on medium-low heat. Add the oil and onions and sauté, stirring occasionally, until translucent, approximately 3 to 5 minutes.

2. Add the salt, black pepper, sweet potatoes and vegetable stock. Bring to a boil, reduce the heat to medium-low and cook for 20 to 25 minutes or until the sweet potatoes are fork-tender.

3. Remove from the heat and cool to room temperature.

4. In the Ninja 24-ounce cup, add all the cooked sweet potato mixture and tofu. Blend the soup mixture for 25 to 30 seconds.

5. Return to the pot and simmer until heated.

1 SERVING: CALORIES 220; FAT 9G; SODIUM 740MG; POTASSIUM 590MG; CARBOHYDRATES 32G; SUGAR 8G; FIBER 5G; PROTEIN 5G; VITAMIN A 380% DV; VITAMIN C 8% DV; MAGNESIUM 15% DV; ZINC 6% DV

Tabbouleh Dip
p. 87

PREP TIME: 10 minutes **YIELD:** 1 cup **CUP SIZE:** 18 ounces

cucumber feta dip

· ·

A delicious and light dip perfect with fresh carrots, peppers, and celery sticks!

ingredients

1 small English cucumber, roughly chopped

¼ small red onion, cut in half

¼ cup loosely packed fresh dill

½ cup crumbled feta cheese

1 tablespoon freshly squeezed lemon juice

¼ teaspoon ground black pepper

directions

1. Place half of the chopped cucumber into the Ninja 18-ounce cup, then add the rest of the ingredients in the order listed, finishing with the other half of the cucumber; pulse 8 to 10 times.

tabbouleh dip

• •

This dip contains parsley, a culinary herb with the same amount of vitamin C as an orange. Plus, it's gluten-free!

ingredients

¾ cup **English cucumber,** cut into quarters

¼ **small yellow onion,** cut into quarters

¼ cup loosely packed **fresh mint,** stems removed

1 cup loosely packed **flat-leaf parsley**

2 **vine-ripe tomatoes,** cut into quarters

½ teaspoon **ground black pepper**

½ teaspoon **kosher salt**

1 tablespoon **extra-virgin olive oil**

3 tablespoons **freshly squeezed lemon juice**

directions

1. Place all the ingredients in the order listed into the Ninja 24-ounce cup and blend for 15 seconds.

PREP TIME: 25 minutes **COOK TIME:** 9 minutes **YIELD:** 1½ cups **CUP SIZE:** 18 ounces

french onion tofu dip

A healthier option without all the added fat, and so delicious!

ingredients

1 tablespoon vegetable oil

1 medium yellow onion, chopped

½ teaspoon kosher salt

¼ teaspoon ground black pepper

3 tablespoons malt vinegar

½ cup firm tofu

4 ounces fat-free cream cheese, softened

⅓ cup fat-free sour cream

directions

1. In a 10-inch sauté pan at medium heat, add the oil, onion, salt and black pepper. Cook for 6 to 8 minutes or until caramelized, stirring occasionally. Add the malt vinegar and cook for 1 minute.

2. Remove from the heat and let cool for 10 minutes.

3. Place the cooked onion mixture, tofu, cream cheese and sour cream into the Ninja 18-ounce cup and blend for 15 seconds or until completely blended.

PREP TIME: 10 minutes **YIELD:** 1¾ cups **CUP SIZE:** 24 ounces

salsa verde

A common Mexican salsa, it ranges in spiciness and may be served warm or cold with tacos, tortilla chips, or even grilled fish.

ingredients

¼ small yellow onion, cut in half

¼ jalapeño, seeded

1 garlic clove, peeled

3 tablespoons flat-leaf parsley

⅓ cup packed fresh cilantro

½ poblano or Anaheim pepper, seeded, cut into chunks

4 tomatillos, peeled, cut into quarters

¼ cup extra-virgin olive oil

1 tablespoon fresh lime juice

¼ teaspoon kosher salt

directions

1. Place all the ingredients in the order listed into the Ninja 24-ounce cup and blend for 15 to 20 seconds.

sauces, dips & more

PREP TIME: 10 minutes **COOK TIME:** 25 minutes **YIELD:** 1¾ cups **CUP SIZE:** 24 ounces

fresh & healthy ketchup relish

A savory topper made from fresh veggies!

ingredients

½ small yellow onion, cut into quarters, plus ¼ small yellow onion, cut in half

½ red bell pepper, seeded, cut into quarters

1 garlic clove, peeled

3 vine-ripe tomatoes, seeded, cut into quarters

1 tablespoon plus 2 teaspoons apple cider vinegar

½ teaspoon molasses

¼ teaspoon ground black pepper

¾ cup baby dill pickles, cut in half

1 tablespoon Dijon mustard

directions

1. Place the ½ small yellow onion, red bell pepper, garlic, tomatoes, apple cider vinegar, molasses and ground black pepper into the Ninja 24-ounce cup and blend for 25 seconds.

2. Pour the tomato mixture into a 2-quart sauce pot and cook on medium heat for 25 minutes, stirring occasionally.

3. Remove from the heat and pour into an airtight container and refrigerate for 1 hour.

4. In the Ninja 24-ounce cup, place the ¼ small yellow onion, pickles, Dijon mustard and the cooled tomato mixture and pulse 6 times.

PREP TIME: 10 minutes **YIELD:** 1¾ cups **CUP SIZE:** 18 ounces

eggless mayonnaise

This vegan mayonnaise is tofu based with a little tang.

ingredients

1½ cups firm tofu, drained, chopped

¼ cup extra-virgin olive oil

½ teaspoon ground black pepper

1 tablespoon Dijon mustard

1 tablespoon plus 1 teaspoon freshly squeezed lemon juice

2 tablespoons apple cider vinegar

directions

1. Place all the ingredients in the order listed into the Ninja 18-ounce cup and blend for 20 seconds.

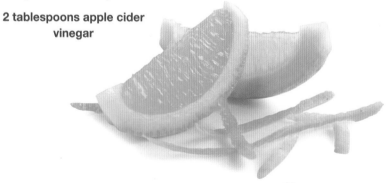

PREP TIME: 10 minutes **YIELD:** 2 cups **CUP SIZE:** 24 ounces

tofu alfredo sauce

Use this tofu-based sauce like you would an Alfredo sauce.

ingredients

1 cup silken tofu

⅓ cup 1-inch cubes Parmesan cheese

⅔ cup unsalted chicken stock

¼ teaspoon ground black pepper

¼ cup packed fresh basil, stems removed

1 garlic clove, peeled

directions

1. Place all the ingredients in the order listed into the Ninja 24-ounce cup and blend for 30 seconds.

PREP TIME: 10 minutes **YIELD:** 1¾ cups **CUP SIZE:** 18 ounces

sauces, dips & more

passion fruit mustard dressing

Perfect for salads or as a marinade for chicken, this dressing is filled with vitamin A and C!

ingredients

½ cup frozen passion fruit pulp, thawed

2 tablespoons Dijon mustard

¼ cup rice wine vinegar

3 tablespoons honey

2 tablespoons fresh thyme

½ teaspoon kosher salt

3 tablespoons extra-virgin olive oil

¾ cup fat-free sour cream

directions

1. Place all the ingredients in the order listed into the Ninja 18-ounce cup and blend for 25 seconds.

NINJA KNOW-HOW SERVE WITH FRESH ARUGULA FOR AN EXTRA VITAMIN B PUNCH.

PREP TIME: 10 minutes   **YIELD:** 1¾ cups   **CUP SIZE:** 18 ounces

berry dressing

A crisp, fruity dressing with tons of extra antioxidants. You will never use the store-bought stuff again!

ingredients

¼ cup fresh blueberries

½ cup fresh strawberries, stems removed

¼ cup fresh raspberries

½ teaspoon ground black pepper

½ teaspoon kosher salt

3 tablespoons raspberry vinegar

⅔ cup extra-virgin olive oil

directions

1. Place all the ingredients in the order listed into the Ninja 18-ounce cup and blend for 35 seconds.

PREP TIME: 15 minutes **YIELD:** 1¼ cups **CUP SIZE:** 18 ounces

everyday vinaigrette

This basic salad dressing recipe is full of nutritional green herbs and none of the preservatives in store-bought dressings.

ingredients

½ cup packed fresh cilantro,
stems removed

⅓ cup packed flat-leaf parsley,
stems removed

2 tablespoons roughly
chopped chives

1 garlic clove, peeled

¼ teaspoon ground black pepper

¼ teaspoon kosher salt

1 tablespoon Dijon mustard

¼ cup apple cider vinegar

¾ cup extra-virgin olive oil

directions

1. Place all the ingredients in the order listed into the Ninja 18-ounce cup and blend for 25 seconds.

sauces, dips & more

avocado caesar dressing

· ·

Avocado adds natural creaminess for a heart-healthy dressing!

ingredients

1 ripe avocado, pitted, cut in half

3 garlic cloves, peeled

1½ ounces Parmesan cheese,
cut into 1-inch pieces

1 ounce oil-cured anchovy filets

½ teaspoon ground black pepper

2 tablespoons freshly squeezed
lemon juice

2 tablespoons apple cider vinegar

1 cup cold water

directions

1. Place all the ingredients in the order listed into the Ninja 18-ounce cup and blend for 30 seconds.

NINJA®
KNOW-HOW
SERVE DRESSING WITH A ROMAINE SALAD; FOR A FULL MEAL, ADD GRILLED CHICKEN BREAST OR SALMON!

PREP TIME: 15 minutes **YIELD:** 2 cups **CUP SIZE:** 18 ounces

supreme goddess dressing

A much healthier version than the classic green goddess dressing. Think outside the box and serve this with steamed asparagus or baked fish.

ingredients

⅓ cup rice wine vinegar

3 garlic cloves, peeled

¼ cup Dijon mustard

½ teaspoon kosher salt

¼ teaspoon ground black pepper

¼ cup light mayonnaise

½ cup flat-leaf parsley

¼ cup fresh tarragon

¼ cup fresh dill, stems removed

2 sprigs scallion, cut into pieces

1 cup fat-free cottage cheese

½ cup extra-virgin olive oil

directions

1. Place all the ingredients in the order listed into the Ninja 18-ounce cup and blend for 25 seconds.

PREP TIME: 5 minutes **COOK TIME:** 15 minutes **YIELD:** 2 cups **CUP SIZE:** 18 ounces

tandoori marinade

This flavorful marinade has anti-inflammatory benefits!

ingredients

2 ounces dried ancho chili
peppers

1 teaspoon fresh ginger

2 garlic cloves, peeled

½ cup fresh cilantro,
stems removed

2 tablespoons garam
masala powder

⅛ teaspoon ground
nutmeg

1 tablespoon freshly
squeezed lemon juice

1 cup nonfat Greek yogurt

½ cup cold water

directions

1. Place the dried ancho chili peppers into a
   small saucepan and pour just enough water
   to cover the peppers. Bring to a boil, reduce
   to a simmer and cook for 10 minutes. Strain
   peppers and then cool.

2. Remove the top and seeds from the
   peppers.

3. Place all the ingredients in the order listed
   into the Ninja 18-ounce cup and blend for
   25 seconds.

Sauces, dips & more

asian marinade

· ·

A flavorful marinade with immunity and anti-inflammatory benefits from this herb combination!

ingredients

⅓ cup mirin

½ cup low-sodium tamari sauce

½ lime, peeled

½ lemon, peeled

½ orange, peeled

1 tablespoon ground coriander

1 tablespoon fresh ginger

3 garlic cloves, peeled

2 sprigs scallion, cut into pieces

directions

1. Place all the ingredients in the order listed into the Ninja 18-ounce cup and blend for 30 seconds.

pineapple cilantro dipping sauce

A healthy and savory sauce that is perfect as a dip or marinade for chicken or fish!

ingredients

½ sweet white onion, peeled,
cut in half

2 tablespoons cilantro leaves

2 tablespoons lime juice

1 tablespoon coconut oil or other oil

½ small Serrano chile, seeded

1 cup pineapple

Salt and pepper to taste

directions

1. Place all the ingredients in the order listed above into the Ninja 18-ounce cup and blend for 15 seconds.

*Tropical Fresh
Fruit Ice Pops*
p. 105

PREP TIME: 5 minutes **YIELD:** 4 servings **CUP SIZE:** 24 ounces

choc-a-lot frappe

Rice milk, tofu and cacao dark chocolate make this a much healthier version than the fast-food chocolate frozen treat.

ingredients

½ cup silken tofu

½ cup 70% cacao dark chocolate

⅔ cup chocolate rice milk

1 (.035 ounce) packet stevia

2 cups ice

directions

1. Place all the ingredients in the order listed into the Ninja 24-ounce cup and blend for 25 seconds.

tropical fresh fruit ice pops

Mango and pineapple make this a tropical treat. With the addition of agave nectar, it is still only 80 calories per pop.

ingredients

1 cup fresh mango

2 cups fresh pineapple

2 tablespoons agave

directions

1. Place all the ingredients in the order listed above into the Ninja 24-ounce cup and blend for 30 seconds. Pour into popsicle molds and freeze overnight or until solid.

PREP TIME: 5 minutes   **YIELD:** 2 servings   **CUP SIZE:** 18 ounces

banana pudding

Vegan, no-cook banana pudding—how easy.

ingredients

1 tablespoon white chia seeds

2 medium frozen bananas, halved

⅓ cup walnut halves

¼ teaspoon ground cinnamon

¼ teaspoon pure vanilla extract

½ cup original flavor rice milk

directions

1. Place the chia seeds in a container and add ⅓ cup water. Cover and place in the refrigerator overnight to soak.

2. Place all the ingredients in the order listed into the Ninja 18-ounce cup and blend for 20 seconds.

PREP TIME: 5 minutes YIELD: 4 servings CUP SIZE: 24 ounces

hawaiian frappe

This dessert is only 70 calories per serving!

ingredients

½ banana

1 cup frozen pineapple chunks

1 cup coconut water

1 tablespoon extra-virgin raw coconut oil

1 cup ice

directions

1. Place all the ingredients in the order listed into the Ninja 24-ounce cup and blend for 30 seconds.

   PREP TIME: 5 minutes   YIELD: 4 servings   CUP SIZE: 24 ounces

vanilla nut frozen treat

Prepare your own frozen dessert guilt-free! Add some fresh berries!

ingredients

⅔ cup vanilla oat milk

½ cup walnut halves

¼ teaspoon pure vanilla extract

1 (.035 ounce) packet stevia

1 6-ounce container nonfat vanilla Greek yogurt

2½ cups ice

directions

1. Place all the ingredients in the order listed into the Ninja 24-ounce cup and blend for 20 seconds.

cherry cheesecake dip

Made with almond butter, containing heart-healthy essential fatty acids, and vitamin C–rich dark cherries, this dip is full of nutrition. Serve with graham crackers!

ingredients

¾ cup dried cherries

1 tablespoon almond milk

1 tablespoon almond butter

1 (.035 ounce) packet stevia

1 8-ounce package fat-free cream cheese, softened

1⅓ cups frozen dark sweet cherries, thawed

directions

1. Place all the ingredients in the order listed into the Ninja 18-ounce cup and pulse 10 times, then blend for 15 seconds.

monkey madness

A healthier version than the frozen "chunky monkey" treat.

ingredients

1 ripe banana, cut in half

2 tablespoons unsweetened cocoa powder

1¼ cups original almond milk

1 tablespoon agave nectar

¼ cup almond butter

1 cup ice

directions

1. Place all the ingredients in the order listed into the Ninja 24-ounce cup and blend for 30 seconds.

NINJA KNOW-HOW | ADD 2 TABLESPOONS CACAO NIBS FOR A SUPER FOOD BOOST.

index

NUTRI NINJA™

Guide to
Nutritional Goodness

75+ delicious recipes

NUTRI NINJA™

Energize Your Life!

Wouldn't it be amazing if you could drink a delicious, natural powerhouse of nutrients fast and easily? The Nutri Ninja™ is your solution. Unlock the hidden vitamins and minerals of whole fruits and vegetables with nutrient complete juicing™. Add nuts, seeds, and herbs for added nutrients and flavors! Use Ninja® Know-How Tips to add a super food boost to your drinks. These recipes have been created based on optimal wellness states to start your journey toward a healthier life. Just one Nutri Ninja™ drink a day can get you started toward a more balanced diet and a healthier lifestyle. You will soon realize that healthy can mean delicious, too!

6 CHAPTERS With 75+ Delicious Recipes

NUTRIENT-RICH JUICES ▪ INFUSED TEAS & WATERS ▪ BREAKFAST
SOUPS & ENTRÉES ▪ SAUCES, DIPS & MORE ▪ DESSERT TREATS

$19.95
ISBN 978-1-4675-9862-0
51995>

9 781467 598620